Get wiser in 10 minutes

How to Build Successful
BUSINESS PARTNERSHIPS

Judy Weintraub

www.skillbites.net

Discover other titles by Judy Weintraub at SkillBites.net:

The Essentials of Negotiating Effectively

TABLE OF CONTENTS

HOW TO BUILD
SUCCESSFUL BUSINESS
PARTNERSHIPS

INTRODUCTION

Everybody has a story about a partnership that has fallen apart. Unfortunately, it is a somewhat common occurrence, as about 2 out of every 3 partnerships fail. Yet entering into partnerships can greatly expand a company's opportunities and markets. This SkillBite discusses how to build durable partner relationships. In particular, it covers:

✓ How to investigate a prospective partner prior to entering into a business alliance;

✓ Key business issues to address up front or as early as possible; and

✓ Critical legal issues to include in a partnership agreement to protect yourself in the event that the partnership doesn't succeed.

While it is most beneficial to conduct an investigation and address the business and legal issues prior to entering into a partnership, it is still worthwhile to go through these steps even after the partnership has been formed. The exercise of discussing the issues will not only help reduce the risk that the partnership will fail, but also enhance the collaboration, communication and alignment of the parties and their interests, thereby strengthening their relationship and the business.

Let me illustrate the value of engaging in this type of exercise with a scenario: Bob and Jack decided to open an online training business together. They had both been in the training business for many years, and between them they knew every aspect of the business. Bob had worked on the marketing and sales side of the business for a large training company, while Jack managed operations in a computer training boutique. They had been good friends for many years and their kids were on the same soccer team.

A year later, they were barely speaking to each other. Jack felt that Bob had not met his commitments to bring in new clients. Bob felt that Jack had spent way too much money developing the product. They both had a lot of money tied up in the business, which was not as successful as they had envisioned.

In the rush to start their business, Bob and Jack never addressed the details of their business relationship; they knew that together they possessed the relevant skills, and figured they could get along with each other well enough to operate the business. Besides, working out the details of the business relationship would have been time consuming, and didn't seem to be important, so they skipped this (critical) step.

As a result of their problems with each other, they stopped communicating, which exacerbated their problems. Decisions that ought to have been made together were being made unilaterally or not at all. They had no agreement that spelled out what would happen if the partnership were to fall apart, or how a partner could exit the partnership. And because they were angry at each other, the negotiations on these issues were bitter.

Unfortunately, Bob and Jack's situation is not that unusual; and yet, it could have been prevented. Partners of failed businesses often admit that had they taken the time to explore the relationship and each other's expectations before jumping into the business, they could have discovered up front the issues that caused the friction leading to their break-up. By working through the types of issues that often cause problems among business principals, prospective partners are better able to prevent the issues from causing them problems. They also are able to develop strategies for overcoming obstacles that are revealed during the discussions, as well as develop systems and procedures in key areas and learn an approach for tackling other tough issues that will inevitably arise.

So congratulations for picking up and reading this book! The time and effort you put in to engage in the discussions recommended in the book with your partner will enable you to minimize the risk of partnership breakdown and build a strong foundation for your partnership.

Preliminary Considerations

Even before you begin doing the exercises covered in the next several chapters, you should think seriously as to whether you truly need or want a partner. What are you looking for in a partner? If you are looking for financial support or expertise in an area that you lack but need, are there other ways to fill the void?

Also, think about bringing your prospective partner on as an employee or contractor for a period of time so you have a chance to evaluate their performance, and determine whether you work well with them. I would suggest at least a 6 month probation period. People are pretty good at being on their best behavior for 3 months; that's harder to do for 6 months or a year.

FAMILY BUSINESSES

Going into business with a family member may seem like a logical step to take. You know each other's strengths and weaknesses, and you get along very well. You may think that you don't need to spend the time to go through the issues and create a formal agreement with a sibling, cousin or offspring. If anything, however, it is even more important to go through the process of addressing business issues and preparing a partnership agreement with prospective partners who are family members than with non-family partners. When the business does not go as well as you had planned, the family relationship is likely to suffer unless the types of issues discussed in this book are addressed; and a damaged family relationship can be considerably more painful than a rupture of a relationship with a non-family partner.

What if a family member starts sloughing off, getting in to work late or taking off early, not getting work done on time or not getting it done in a quality manner? If you were dealing with a normal employee, you might discipline the employee or even terminate him; but if it's your mother, or your brother, how do you handle that?

What if your partner is your daughter and she wants to start working part time and/or bringing your baby grandchild into the office? As a parent, you want your daughter to spend time raising your grandchild, but as a partner, you need her to focus on her work.

What if your partner is your father, and he keeps making unilateral decisions that you don't agree with, and which are in your area of authority? One family business nearly caused a father and son to stop talking with each other when the father hired a senior executive without the son's knowledge or input.

As a partner in a family business, you wear at least 2 hats – your business hat and your family hat. You need to set up a system that allows you to wear your business hat when dealing with family issues that affect the business, and make sure that every family member in the business (whether they are a partner or not) understands the system.

In family businesses, it is critical to have a strong communication system for discussing both business and family issues. One family business I worked with, owned by a mother and her two daughters, held weekly meetings every Friday at 4 pm, where they went over what went well and what didn't during the week and planned for the coming week during the first half hour, and the second half hour was reserved to discuss any relationship issue or concern that one of them felt a need to air.

Take the time to address the issues discussed in this book. Read other books or articles on good family business practices. Your family relationships are too important to risk jeopardizing by not spending the time establishing expectations, goals, roles and responsibilities, decision-making guidelines and other critical business issues.

INVESTIGATING YOUR PROSPECTIVE PARTNER

How well do you know your prospective partner? If your partner is your brother or sister, you probably don't have to spend a lot of time on this section. But even if you have been good friends with this person for a long time, you may not know whether they have any skeletons in the closet that could concern you. For instance, what if you were to discover that your childhood friend had a DWI (driving while intoxicated) on his record, or had a poor credit report? Depending on the circumstances, you might not be concerned; but it is better to know about the skeletons (if any) in advance, than to find out about them after you've brought the person into your business.

A partnership is like a marriage. You will spend a lot of time with your partner, sometimes even more than you will with your spouse. Your reputation and your investment in the business will be on the line, so before you enter into the partnership, make sure you know as much about your prospective partner as possible.

The investigation of a person's background, sometimes referred to as due diligence, involves a number of different components which can vary, depending on the circumstances. You might start with verifying some of the credentials on the person's resume: did they go to the schools and work at the companies listed? Do they have the skills they've identified?

You might also want to conduct a credit check, particularly if the person you are bringing in is going to have access to your funds and/or handle any financial matters for you. Do you want to bring in a partner whose credit report shows that they are late in paying their bills or have a lot of debt?

Another part of the background check is to conduct a legal review. Find out if they have a criminal record, or if there are any lawsuits pending against them, or any liens filed against them, such as for back taxes.

If the business will require any driving, you might also want to check with the motor vehicles department. If you are running a transportation company, for example, you may not want a partner with a lot of moving violations.

Note that you can outsource background checks to companies that perform this service. You can expect to pay about $100 for the credit check, legal review and motor vehicle department review.

To the extent that you can, try to talk with former business colleagues and personal friends of the person. Find out about your prospective partner's reputation, interests, personality, integrity – basically, you want to verify that this person is someone you will feel comfortable working with for a long time.

You may also want to find out about their family situation. Does the person's spouse or significant other support them in their desire to enter into the partnership? Does the spouse understand the expectations for the business? In one case involving two women partners, the husband of one of them turned out to be against his wife's involvement, which became abundantly evident when the business started to become successful, requiring more of her time. Ultimately, the partnership broke apart, as she decided to leave the business rather than risk jeopardizing her marriage.

Finally, you could ask your prospective partner to complete some assessment forms, to give you a better sense of their abilities, personality, communications preferences and the like. For instance, there are assessment tools to determine whether someone is suitable for entrepreneurship. The SBA has a free assessment tool on its website at http://www.sba.gov/content/use-our-starting-assessment-tool. A person who comes from a large corporation may have a hard time adjusting to the roller-coaster of entrepreneurship. An assessment can help determine whether they can handle the financial and emotional risks.

Other assessment tools can help you understand the person's approach to making decisions, handling stress or chaos, and dealing with criticism. For instance, you and your partner could each take the entrepreneur strength assessment offered in *The One Minute Entrepreneur*, authored by Ken Blanchard (do a search for The One Minute Entrepreneur to find the free download). This assessment tool is designed to identify areas of competency as well as areas needing improvement. You might learn, for example, that your prospective partner generally likes to make quick decisions and doesn't like spending time analyzing data. If you are the same way, this could spell trouble. It is not to say that you shouldn't consider them as a partner, but it does suggest that you would be wise to determine some way of balancing this behavior with certain checks to make sure you aren't entering into things too hastily.

There are many different kinds of assessment tools you can find on the internet. The more you can learn about your prospective partner, the better able you will be to determine whether this person is truly suitable to be your partner.

ADDRESS KEY
BUSINESS ISSUES

Assuming you have gotten over the first hurdle and determined that there is nothing in the person's background that concerns you, the next step is to make sure you are compatible with each other and aligned on key strategic issues. Compatibility consists of more than just being able to get along with each other. It also encompasses such elements as your expectations, values, and strengths and weaknesses.

One of the main causes of partnership failure is unmet expectations. I see a lot of partners who are bitter because they do not feel their co-partner is working as hard at the business as they are. They are putting in 80 hours per week, while the co-partner is putting in significantly fewer hours. What started out as a minor annoyance grows into a major conflict.

There's a long list of expectations that partners ought to explore with each other besides the number of working hours that each partner expects to spend on the business. Some other discussion points include:

- ✓ Financial expectations (e.g., desired salary in the short term, interim and long term; desired age for retirement)
- ✓ Job performance (how will performance be measured; how will partners hold each other accountable)
- ✓ Communications (how often, what means)
- ✓ Office etiquette (dress code, office hours, work habits, responsiveness, punctuality)
- ✓ Vacation and sick leave
- ✓ Family commitments
- ✓ Religious restrictions

This is only a sample of the types of issues that could be discussed. Not all of these will be pertinent in every situation, and depending on the circumstances, there could be others that ought to be included.

Another component of compatibility consists of determining whether your value system is compatible with your partner's value system. If you value high quality, for instance, and your partner values low price, you can foresee that there will be conflicts in how you run the business. There are worksheets that can help you prioritize your values, which you can then compare with the prioritized list of your partner. A highly reputable values assessment tool called the Hall-Tonna Values Assessment is discussed and provided in the book *Values Shift*, by Brian Hall (available on Amazon)

You don't have to have the same values to be compatible. The exercise is intended more to open your eyes to possible issues so that you can determine how important the issues are and whether there is a way to minimize your risk.

Similarly, you should each identify your strengths and weaknesses. If you both have the same weakness, you'll want to figure out how to compensate for that weakness. For example, if neither of you has any financial savvy, you could both get some training, or appoint one of you to get trained, or decide to rely on your accountant (not a recommended course of action).

Another critical area to address is your approach on key business issues. For instance, what are the goals of the business? Each of you should identify the 3 to 5 year goals for the business. If you aren't aligned here, that could be a major problem.

How will equity be allocated? Will you be 50/50 partners, or will one partner own more than the other? How will you value each person's nonmonetary contributions into the company? For example, if one person puts in sweat equity, how will you value their time?

Other key issues to address include the following:

- ✓ What will be each person's role in the company?
- ✓ How will decisions be made? What decisions require joint approval, and what decisions can be made unilaterally?
- ✓ How will the partners be compensated for the work they perform for the venture?
- ✓ When will profits be distributed, and to what extent will they be plowed back into the company?
- ✓ How much debt is each partner willing to incur?

Further, you should conduct some scenario planning, where you anticipate possible situations the business could encounter and develop strategies for managing those situations. For instance, what if a major competitor comes into your area? What if your business does phenomenally well? Will you expand into different geographic markets? What if someone wants to buy you out? Not only will this exercise help you determine whether you will be able to work well with your prospective partner, but it will also help you deal with various situations when they do arise.

To obtain a handy checklist of issues to address with your partner, go to http://skillbites. net/partnershipissues/. There are a few different approaches you can take: you could each write down your views on the various issues you want to address, and then meet to share your views and discuss them. Alternatively, you could use an attorney or other business advisor to facilitate the discussion. Someone who has years of experience with partnerships can probe into your answers, uncover other important issues and help you develop systems and processes to minimize problems.

I recommend that you document the results of your discussion, and repeat this exercise every few years. Things can change over time, and the document might need to be updated. If you find that your prospective partner is having trouble finding the time to work on this, or is uncomfortable discussing his or her views, take that as a warning signal of potential problems ahead.

PROTECT YOURSELF WITH A PARTNERSHIP AGREEMENT

If you are going into business with a partner, or even if you have been in business with a partner for some time, it is important to have a partnership agreement in place. This agreement is referred to as a shareholder agreement or buy/sell agreement in a corporation, or an operating agreement in a limited liability company. For simplicity purposes, the agreement will be referred to generically as a partnership agreement.

There are many reasons why you need to have a partnership agreement. Some of the main reasons include the following:

✓ To protect yourself in the event that the partnership doesn't work well. You will want to have a defined process for dissolving the partnership, and for one partner buying out the other partner. You will also want to define who owns what, and other important rights and obligations.

✓ To document key issues such as the equity allocation among the owners, how the business will be managed, how decisions will be made, voting rights, meetings, roles and responsibilities and the like.

✓ To control the transfer of ownership. Without this type of agreement, your partner could sell his or her interest in the company to someone whom you would prefer not to have as a partner. Or your partner may encumber his or her interest (that is, use it as collateral for a loan), and if the partner later defaulted on the loan, you could find yourself in a partnership with the lender.

✓ To spell out exit strategies. If one of you leaves the business for any reason, this agreement would define how you will value the ownership interest to pay off the departing owner and the payment terms. The agreement will also identify the circumstances under which the remaining owners and company have the right to buy out the departing owner, and any circumstances under which the departing owner can force the remaining owners and company to buy out their interest. These are issues that are best addressed early in the life of the business, when the partners are still friends. As can be imagined, it is considerably more difficult to reach a resolution on these issues after the partners have opposing interests.

I recommend that you retain the services of an attorney who has considerable experience in drafting partnership agreements to help you prepare your agreement. While you can download an agreement template from the internet and customize it to your needs, this is dangerous. You don't know whether the template you have used contains all of the appropriate provisions, and if you don't understand it, you won't know whether to or how to revise it to fit your needs. There are books you can buy that will guide you through the contract terms; however, there could be adverse tax consequences in your circumstance that might not be evident from reading a book, that an attorney could help minimize. You should plan on spending $2500 to $5000 for the preparation of a partnership agreement.

It is a good idea to have a basic understanding of what should be included in a partnership agreement so that you can make informed decisions regarding how to structure your partnership agreement so that it fits your needs. I've provided an overview of the major issues below. To obtain a list of the issues to include in a partnership agreement, visit http://skillbites.net/partnershipagreementissues/.

1. Limiting the Transfer of Ownership Interests

Do you want to limit the ability of an owner to transfer her interest? Do you want to prohibit any transfer of ownership interest? This gives you the greatest control, but it can cause problems, as there may be certain circumstances which would cause a hardship to an existing owner if he were unable to transfer his interest. For instance, an owner may really need the cash.

A typical provision in partnership agreements is to give the company and continuing owner(s) a Right of First Refusal when an owner considers transferring his or her ownership interest. The company and continuing owners would then have the ability to evaluate the prospective buyer and determine whether they would prefer to have the buyer as an owner or to spend the money to buy back the departing owner's interest.

You could allow the majority owner to transfer her interest without obtaining consent or being restricted by a right of first refusal, but impose a right of first refusal on any minority owners. In fact, with regard to any of the issues, you can set different standards for minority owners and the majority owner. I do not repeat this for the other issues, but it should be kept in mind.

2. Providing the Right to Force Buyouts

Sometimes, events occur to one owner that can upset the functioning of a small, closely managed company, and the other owners may want to force the affected owner to sell his or her interest. For instance, if an owner gets divorced or dies or goes bankrupt and his interest is about to be transferred to others, the company may want to require the new owner to sell the interest back to the company.

3. Right of owner to force a sale

There are some situations which may arise where an owner really needs to sell her interest but cannot find a suitable buyer. For instance, if an owner becomes disabled, she may have significant medical expenses and no salary, and needs the money from the sale of her interest; but there may be no market for a minority stake in a family business. To protect the interests of individual owners, you may want to allow them to force the company to buy their ownership interest in certain circumstances. The main circumstances where you might want to allow this are:

a. When an active owner retires or leaves the business;

b. When an owner becomes disabled; and

c. When an owner dies (giving the estate, trust or inheritors the right to force a sale).

4. Buyout Procedure

When an event occurs that triggers either a forced buyout or a right of first refusal, the agreement should spell out what the procedure is: who has the buyout right or right of first refusal, how much time do they have to exercise the right, how notices are sent, etc.

The structure that provides the most flexibility is for the company to have a period of time to exercise the buyout right or right of first refusal, and if it doesn't exercise the right, then the continuing owners have an opportunity to decide whether to buy out the departing owner. Sometimes there are tax advantages for the individual owners to buy back the interest that are not available to the company, and sometimes individual partners can afford the purchase whereas the company cannot.

5. Buyout Price

There are various approaches that can be used to determine the buyout price. The worst approach is not to define how the price will be determined, since the departing owner will want a high price and the continuing owners will want a low price. To avoid conflict, and to help from an estate tax standpoint, it is best to spell out what the buyout price will be in the various circumstances, or at least how it is to be determined. Your accountant or lawyer should be able to suggest an approach that will work for you and your partners.

Here are the 5 most common approaches for setting the buyout price:

a. **Fixed Price.** This provides certainty and simplicity, and allows you to know how much insurance to buy to fund a buyout. The disadvantage is figuring out a fair fixed price, as the fair value may change over time. To keep the price fair, you would need to provide for periodic adjustments.

b. **Book Value.** This is also a simple method, but it does not take into account the value of intangible assets such as goodwill, intellectual property, mailing lists or a desirable location, and thus is usually lower than true value. For new businesses, this is an appropriate method.

c. **Multiple of Book Value.** This method uses a multiplier to increase the value of assets to take into account the value of the business' intangible assets. The difficulty is in determining the appropriate multiplier.

d. **Capitalization of Earnings.** This approach measures a business's value by its profits. It is calculated by multiplying the business's profit (average profit over several years, such as 5) by a multiplier. It is appropriate for well established businesses. Business appraisers and brokers are a good source for determining the appropriate multiplier.

e. **Appraisal Value.** This method defines the buyout price by the value determined by an independent appraisal. It is easy, but it can be expensive and time consuming, and it does not permit you to know the price in advance, so neither the departing owner nor the continuing owners know what to expect or how to plan. If this method is chosen, it is important to choose an appraiser in advance, someone with expertise in your industry, and define the amount of time for the appraisal to take.

If estate planning is an issue for any partner, that partner might want to talk to an estate planner about the buyout price. The higher the buyout price, the more one's heirs will have to pay in taxes, if the partner still owns a portion of the company at his death. Just remember that a low price will apply in other circumstances besides death, such as when a partner wants to retire. As long as you select a price that can be substantiated, the IRS will generally accept whatever price is stipulated in your agreement.

Note that you can vary the buyout price, depending on the circumstances. For instance, you could set one price if an owner becomes disabled, retires or dies, and a lower price if an owner quits after working in the business fewer than, say, 5 years, and another lower price if a partner is fired.

6. Payment Terms

These are arguably the most important provisions in the partnership agreement. The buyer, who is either the company or the continuing owners, usually wants to pay a small amount up front and the rest over an extended time period. The seller, who is either the departing owner, her family or estate, wants more up front and to receive the balance fairly quickly. The negotiations on the payment terms directly affect the purchase price, as the buyer may be able to pay more if the payments are extended, or the seller may be willing to accept less if a lump sum payment is made, or payments are made over a short period of time.

It is important to try to come up with a formula that is affordable to the company and continuing owners as well as being fair to the departing owner. If the company cannot afford the payment terms, it may be prevented from being able to buy back an owner's interest. On the other hand, if the payments are over many years, the departing owner or her family could incur substantial hardship as well as the risk that something happens to the business and the payments don't get made.

One of the most common payment plans consists of a down payment and then installment payments. Typically, a down payment is made within a specified period after the appropriate notice is given concerning the purchase of the ownership interest, and then installment payments are made over a specified period of time. The higher the down payment, the more acceptable a longer installment period will be. When the installment payments are stretched over more than a year, the agreement usually contains an interest charge on the installment payments. Insurance proceeds can be used to fund the down payment for the purchase of the ownership interest of a deceased or disabled owner.

7. Funding the Buyout

If you don't address how you will fund the buyouts, then your buyout provisions might not have much value. Here are the three most common ways to fund the buyouts.

a. **Cash.** This is the simplest method, but there is always a risk that the company or continuing owners will not have enough cash when the time comes.

b. **Borrowing.** This is also easy, but may not be practicable, as the company and continuing owners may not have good credit at the time they need to borrow money, or interest rates might be much higher than at the time the agreement was executed, making borrowing less affordable.

c. **Insurance.** This is available to cover buyouts due to death or disability, but usually not for other factors. It can also be expensive, although it is generally cheaper than simply saving the money that would otherwise be used for the premiums. This is a complicated area with lots of issues, such as who buys the insurance, what type of insurance to buy, making sure the face value keeps up with the value of the ownership interest, and various tax ramifications. It is important to discuss these issues with an insurance agent or broker familiar with partnership agreements and/or a qualified financial planner or CPA.

8. Dissolution of the Partnership

The agreement should provide some process for dissolving the business in the event that the partners agree to end the business or the partnership is unsuccessful or other event triggers the need to dissolve. Three important issues to address are (a) what events trigger dissolution, besides agreement of the partners; (b) who is responsible for taking what actions (e.g., informing creditors, vendors and customers, selling assets, finishing contracts); and (c) who owns the name of the business and other intellectual property.

9. Miscellaneous Issues

The partnership agreement typically contains a number of additional provisions. One of these that you should pay attention to is the dispute resolution clause. Disputes often arise between partners, so it is a good idea to include a structured procedure for resolving disputes in the partnership agreement (as well as any other type of agreement). I recommend using a two-step process: begin with mediation, which is much less expensive than litigation, more expeditious, amicable and fair. Then, if the dispute isn't resolved through mediation, proceed to arbitration.

Some other provisions that are commonly included in partnership agreements cover how the business will be managed, the roles and responsibilities of the partners and how decisions will be made.

10. Tax Issues

When an owner sells her ownership interest, there are certain tax consequences concerning the proceeds of the sale. Similarly, there are estate tax consequences when an owner dies and leaves her ownership interest to others. It is important to seek counsel from an accountant or estate tax attorney to understand these tax consequences, and learn some of the ways the partnership agreement can be structured to minimize income and estate taxes.

SUMMARY

Whether you are considering taking on a new partner or are already in a partnership arrangement, it is worth taking some time to evaluate your relationship and make sure your partnership will be built on a good foundation. This includes:

1. Conducting a thorough background check;

2. Understanding each partner's expectations regarding the relationship as well as the business;

3. Determining whether you and your partner are compatible, and are in alignment on major strategic issues; and

4. Entering into a partnership agreement that covers what happens if the partnership doesn't succeed, or one partner wants out.

Every few years, it is worth reviewing these to make sure they still accurately reflect the current views of the partners, and if not, to update them accordingly.

ADDITIONAL RESOURCES

Azriela Jaffe is the co-author of "See Jane Collaborate, Your Essential Guide to Joyful and Prosperous Business Partnerships" (Jane out of the Box Media, 2011), as well as author of the earlier version, *Let's Go Into Business Together: 8 Secrets to Successful Business Partnering,* Career Press 2001, from which some of this source material was drawn. For a more detailed guide to creating a successful partnership, visit http://www.seejanecollaborate. com/.

Nolo Press has a publication called *Business Buyout Agreements*, by Anthony Mancuso and Bethany K. Laurence, June 2010. It contains an explanation of the various provisions to include in a partnership agreement and provides a form agreement that can be customized.

ABOUT THE AUTHOR

Judy Weintraub is an attorney with over 30 years legal experience. She runs Weintraub Legal Services, a law firm providing corporate legal services to businesses in the mid-Atlantic region, including partnership workshops and the development of operating agreements, buy-sell agreements and partnership agreements. Ms. Weintraub is also a mediator and arbitrator, serving on the rosters of the American Arbitration Association and the International Institute for Conflict Prevention and Resolution (CPR).

Connect with Judy online:

judy@weintraublegal.com

www.weintraublegal.com

http://www.linkedin.com/pub/judy-weintraub/7/2a9/bb1

Discover other titles by Judy Weintraub at www. SkillBites.net:

The Essentials of Negotiating Effectively

www.ingramcontent.com/pod-product-compliance
Lightning Source LLC
Chambersburg PA
CBHW071545170526
45166CB00004B/1556